HISTORY

The name Shih Tzu (pronounced "sheed zoo"), given to the breed by the Chinese, means Tibetan Lion Dog. It must not be imagined that the Chinese were greatly perturbed by the presence of lions or that they bred these little dogs for the purpose of slaying lions. The most widely accepted theory as to the origin of the name "Lion Dog" is that the breed, when suitably combed and trimmed, could be made up into a creditable representation of a miniature lion.

There are several breeds of short-faced long-haired Asiatic "Lion Dogs" whose lineages go back many centuries. These include such breeds as the Shih Tzu, Lhasa Apso, and Pekingese (and, possibly, the Japanese Chin). Another breed with similar body conformation, but lacking the long hair, is the Pug.

"Lion Dogs," unlike so many other breeds in China, were protected throughout their lives, accorded very high honor, and guarded by eunuchs and even by the army. They were kept in the best part of the Imperial Palace, they slept upon the richest silk, and they fed from the Emperor's personal table.

During the Manchu Dynasty (founded in 1583) it was the custom of the Dalai Lama of Tibet to send propitiatory presents of highly-prized Apsos to the powerful Emperor of China. In addition, Manchu generals who returned from successful invasions of Tibet during the 18th century made a practice of bringing these dogs back as spoils of war. Such dogs were placed, with great ceremony, at the feet of the Emperor as symbols of Manchu victories by junior officers who had played the more successful roles in the campaign. The foundation stock of the Shih Tzu was probably these Tibetan Apsos of the Chinese royal palace

This Shih Tzu puppy proudly poses in front of a silk tapestry depicting his Oriental ancestry.

It is believed that the Shih Tzu from Tibet were on occasion interbred with the native Pekingese. It is apparent that this cross-breeding was done to produce different types and colors as well as to sometimes reduce the size of the Shih Tzu.

and the native Chinese Pekingese.

Crossbreeding, however, may have been more extensive than has been generally imagined, and whether or not this was intentional is uncertain. In the Imperial Palace of Peking there were other short-faced dogs in addition to the Imperial Pekingese. One of these was the smooth-coated breed that was the forerunner of our modern Pug. The Pug is reputed to have been used to breed the original bull-fighting Bulldog down to the squat, scowling gentleman we know today. Unlikely as it may seem that there should be any relationship between Shih Tzu

and the Bulldog, this becomes far less extraordinary when one compares the body of the Shih Tzu beneath its heavy coat of hair with that of the modern Bulldog. One has only in the mind's eye to diminish the size of the Bulldog and provide it with a heavy coat to recognize a likeness between the two breeds.

THE SHIH TZU IN LEGEND AND HISTORY

The earliest record of the Shih Tzu appears in documents dating back to 624 AD. As far as we know, the first mention of these small dogs is made in the Tang Dynasty when K'iu Wen T'ai, King of Viqur, offered to the Chinese

The Shih Tzu's Tibetan heritage is surely demonstrated by its appearance and by its close similarity—in certain respects—to the Lhasa Apso, which also hails from that country.

court a pair of dogs (male and female) in 624 AD. They were said to come from the Fu Lin (probably the Byzantine Empire) and it was then, for the first time that there were dogs of Fu Lin in China. Mention is again made in the period 990-994 AD, when people of the Ho Chou (Ssueh-Van were presented to the Emperors Chien Lung and K'Ang Hsi as well as other Chinese sovereigns as a flattering reminder of the Lamaist Association of the Dynastic Name with Manjusri, the God of Learning, who was habitually accompanied by a small pet dog, which he could transform into a

The Empress Dowager of China, seated, surrounded by her attendants. The imperial eunuch appears in center background.

province) sent dogs as tribute. They were small, of an intelligent mind, constantly tame and docile. They would sit at the sides of the Imperial Couch where at every audience, they were to wag their tails and bark.

Another theory of the introduction of the breed into China is that these dogs were brought from Tibet as tribute to the Chinese court in 1644. They mighty lion to be used as his steed. These dogs were bred in the Forbidden City of Peking and many pictures of them were kept in the Imperial Dog Book. All colors were permissible, but the honey, yellow and golden colors were the favorites of the Old Dowager Empress, yellow being the Imperial Color.

Since the smallest of these dogs resembled a lion, as represented in Oriental art, and in the Buddhist belief there is an association between the lion and their deity, the dogs sent to China would have been selected with care as the finest of their kind. From these dogs developed the Shih Tzu, called by the Chinese the Chrysanthemum-faced Dog because of the manner in which the hair of the face grows, somewhat resembling the flower.

There were humorous as well as loveable qualities about these little mops of taffy-colored silken hair that appealed to the Chinese and aroused their sentiments. These lion dogs, like the Pekingese, were the product of countless generations of careful breeding. Being especially bred to resemble the semi-mythical Buddhist lion as the Chinese imagined him, these dogs were thought to share that mystic creature's formidable power.

Marco Polo records that in the Yuan Dynasty (1206-1333), lions roamed the Courts of the Peking Palace. Emperors paraded leopards, bears, elephants, and finally the lion before their guests on the "10,000 Year Hill." The lions were astonishingly like the little golden-coated dogs bred in Peking. When the first Shih Tzu were brought to the Imperial Court in Peking, the Old Dowager Empress kept them well apart from her favorites, the Pekingese, and their breeding was severely controlled, as she considered them very costly treasures from Tibet. The custom ceased in 1908 with the death of the Dowager Empress.

The Lotus Court at the Summer Palace outside Peking. Generation after generation of Shih Tzu shared in the life of the court.

The courtyard of the Imperial Palace, Peking. For many centuries only the privileged few were allowed access here. It was here that the eunuchs conducted the breeding programs that brought about the regal Shih Tzu.

During the Chinese Revolution many of these dogs were destroyed. Later, and for many years, the Chinese bred them but steadfastly refused to sell them. As late as 1937 there was a common belief that, although the Chinese were at last willing to sell their Shih Tzu, they did not want them to leave the country and would put powdered glass in their food before they left. There may have been some basis of truth in this, as most Shih Tzu taken out of the country died within a short time.

CHINESE GROOMING METHODS

The Shih Tzu's coat came mainly from the Tibetan Apsos and partly from the Pekingese; the lion-like shape was probably accentuated by crosses with the short-haired Puglike form.

It is recorded that the Chinese not only gave the newly produced breed the title of "Shih Tzu" but also made further efforts to make the resemblance more realistic by means of the "lion clip." To accomplish this they left all the hair on the head and shoulders and clipped the hair on the rest of the body close.

In the Chinese Imperial Palace at Peking, the care of these dogs was in the hands of eunuchs who devoted a great deal of time to grooming and tending their charges. It was their custom, apparently, to comb out the dogs' beards and moustaches away from the face and rough up the hair behind the head and on the shoulders to form a lion-like mane. The "chrysanthemum" growth of hair from the upper surface of the nose would then be plaited into the hair that descended from the forehead. The result was that the face became completely hidden beneath a mop of hair that covered the eyes and made it almost impossible for the dog to see anything at all unless peepholes were provided in front of the eyes.

eunuchs in producing such dogs and dressing their coats in the fashion of the times are still to be found in the hands of collectors.

THE ARRIVAL OF THE SHIH TZU IN BRITAIN AND AMERICA

It was not until 1930 that the first pair of Shih Tzu was imported into England by General Sir Douglas and Lady Brownrigg. These were a dog, Hibou, and a

Mrs. Charlotte Kauffman with her black Shih Tzu Schauder and the gold and white Leidza. These two dogs, the first to arrive in Norway, were originally registered as Lhasa Terriers in 1940. Mrs. Kauffman was one of the pioneer breeders in that country.

When the grooming had been successfully done, the court artists were engaged to produce illuminated scrolls depicting the most outstanding examples not only of the breed but also of the art of the court hairdresser. It was considered a very great honor when the picture of some particularly remarkable specimen was recorded in the Imperial Dog Book. A number of illuminated scrolls depicting the success of the

bitch, Shu-Ssa. It was also in 1930 that Miss Hutchins imported into Ireland Lung-Fu-Ssu, a male. In 1934 the Shih Tzu Club was founded, with the Countess of Essex as its president and Lady Brownrigg as secretary. The first Championships were awarded in 1940. Some dissatisfaction was expressed around this time about the size of the dogs, and in 1956 the Manchu Shih Tzu Club was formed, a private society desirous of looking after the interests of the smaller type more in keeping with those originally bred in the palace at Peking. In 1958 the Shih Tzu Club of England agreed to permit its standard to include smaller specimens.

There is no record of any Shih Tzu reaching the United States much before 1950, although some claim that introductions were made about the time that they first arrived in England. If so, the records are no longer available. A considerable number reached the United States from 1950 onward, not only from England but also from France, Sweden, and Denmark. In 1955 the American Kennel Club recognized the Shih Tzu as a distinct breed and allowed them to be shown in the Miscellaneous Class. In 1957 the American Shih Tzu Club came into being. The American Kennel Club agreed that until such time as the A.K.C. permits registry of the Shih Tzu, the English standard of show points should be adopted. Between 1930 and 1960, more than 1,300 Shih Tzu were registered in England. There

The Royal Family relaxing with their dogs at Windsor. The Queen Mother (right) holds Choo-Choo the Shih Tzu, who was bred by Mrs. Charlotte Kauffman.

were about 300 Shih Tzu in the United States at the end of 1963.

Some of the later importations into Britain following the earliest already mentioned included Tashi cf Chouette, a bitch imported by the Earl of Essex in 1938, and Choo-Choo, a dog presented by the Danish Ministry to H.M. Queen Elizabeth, the Queen Mother, in 1933, while she was the Duchess of York. Other importations were three bitches, all imported by General Telfer-Smollet: Ming, in 1939; Ishuh Tzu, in 1948; and Hsing Ehr, in 1952, and Mrs. M. Longden introduced Jungfaltets Yung-Ming from Sweden in 1959.

The reason the Shih Tzu was not heard of earlier is that it was almost impossible to obtain one during the reigns of the Chinese emperors; the dogs were the personal property of the royal family, and anyone attempting to acquire one by unlawful means was promptly put to death. The Lhasa Apso, very similar or possibly identical to the progenitor of the Shih Tzu, reached Britain through India from Tibet.

HEAD
Carried high.
In balance
with the rest
of the body.

HEIGHT 9-10
inches at
withers
(shoulders).

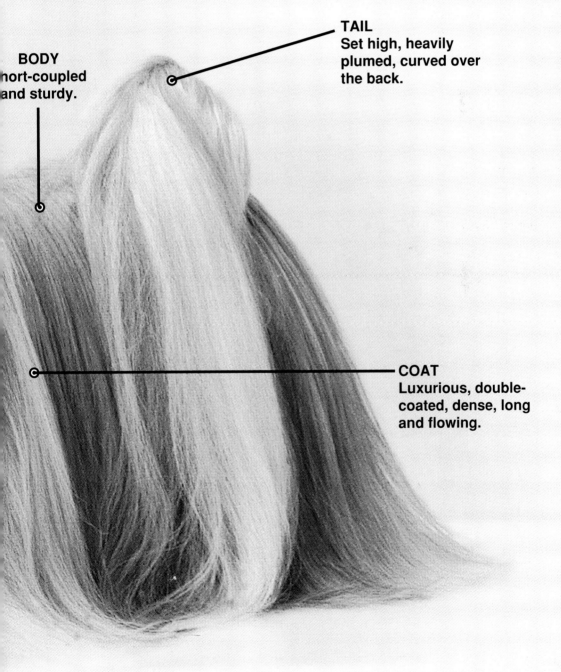

1995 Westminster Kennel Club Best of
Breed Winner Ch. Ista's Wicked Fantasy
owned by Tammarie and Gregory Larson
and Susan Bletzinger.

TAIL
Set high, heavily
plumed, curved over
the back.

BODY
Short-coupled
and sturdy.

COAT
Luxurious, double-
coated, dense, long
and flowing.

STANDARD FOR THE SHIH TZU

A breed standard is the criterion by which the appearance (and to a certain extent, the temperament as well) of any given dog is made subject to objective measurement. Basically, the standard for any breed is a definition of the perfect dog to which all specimens of the breed are compared. Breed standards are always subject to change through review by the national breed club for each dog, so that it is always wise to keep up with developments in a breed by checking the publications of your national kennel club. Printed below is the American Kennel Club Standard for the Shih Tzu.

The Shih Tzu is a solid, sturdy, compact dog, with a long flowing double coat.

the back. Although there has always been considerable size variation, the Shih Tzu must be compact, solid, carrying good weight and substance.

Even though a toy dog, the Shih Tzu must be subject to the same requirements of soundness and structure prescribed for all breeds, and any deviation from the ideal described in the standard should be penalized to the extent of the deviation. Structural faults common to all breeds are as undesirable in the Shih Tzu as in any other breed, regardless of whether or not such faults are specifically mentioned in the standard.

General Appearance—The Shih Tzu is a sturdy, lively, alert toy dog with long flowing double coat. Befitting his noble Chinese ancestry as a highly valued, prized companion and palace pet, the Shih Tzu is proud of bearing, has a distinctively arrogant carriage with head well up and tail curved over

Size, Proportion, Substance—**Size**—Ideally, height at withers is 9 to 10 inches; but, not less than 8 inches nor more than 11 inches. Ideally, weight of mature dogs, 9 to 16 pounds. **Proportion**—Length between withers and root of tail is slightly longer than height at withers. The Shih Tzu must never be so high stationed as to appear leggy, nor so low stationed as to appear dumpy or squatty. **Substance**—Regardless of size, the Shih Tzu is always compact, solid and carries good weight and substance.

and expression rather than an image created by grooming technique. **Eyes**—Large, round, not prominent, placed well apart, looking straight ahead. Very dark. Lighter on liver pigmented dogs and blue pigmented dogs. **Fault:**

The Shih Tzu's expression is warm, sweet, wide-eyed, friendly, and trusting. An overall well-balanced and pleasant expression supercedes the importance of the individual parts that make up the expression itself.

Head—**Head**—Round, broad, wide between eyes, its size in balance with the overall size of the dog being neither too large nor too small. **Fault**: Narrow head, close-set eyes. **Expression**—Warm, sweet, wide-eyed, friendly and trusting. An overall well-balanced and pleasant expression supercedes the importance of individual parts. *Care should be taken to look and examine well beyond the hair to determine if what is seen is the actual head*

Small, close-set or light eyes; excessive eye white. **Ears**—Large, set slightly below crown of skull; heavily coated. **Skull**—Domed. **Stop**—There is a definite stop. **Muzzle**—Square, short, unwrinkled, with good cushioning, set no lower than bottom eye rim; never downturned. Ideally, no longer than 1 inch from tip of nose to stop, although length may vary slightly in relation to overall size of dog. Front of muzzle should be flat; lower lip and chin not protruding and definitely never receding. **Fault**: Snipiness, lack of definite stop. **Nose**—Nostrils are broad, wide and open. **Pigmentation**—Nose, lips, eye rims are black on all colors, except liver on liver pigmented dogs and blue on blue pigmented dogs. **Fault:** Pink on nose, lips or eye rims. **Bite**—Undershot. Jaw is broad and wide. A missing tooth

Body—Short-coupled and sturdy with no waist or tuck-up. The Shih Tzu is slightly longer than tall. **Fault:** Legginess. **Chest**—Broad and deep with good spring of rib, however, not barrel-chested. Depth of rib cage should extend to just below elbow. Distance from elbow to withers is a little greater than from elbow to ground. **Croup**—Flat. **Tail**—Set on high, heavily plumed, carried

The hair on top of the Shih Tzu's head is tied up: this is what is known as the topknot. Owners usually accessorize this feature with brightly colored bows. Drawing by John Quinn.

or slightly misaligned teeth should not be too severely penalized. Teeth and tongue should not show when mouth is closed. **Fault:** Overshot bite.

Neck, Topline, Body—Of utmost importance is an overall well-balanced dog with no exaggerated features. **Neck**—Well set-on flowing smoothly into shoulders; of sufficient length to permit natural high head carriage and in balance with height and length of dog. **Topline**—Level.

in curve well over back. Too loose, too tight, too flat, or too low set a tail is undesirable and should be penalized to extent of deviation.

Forequarters—Shoulders—Well angulated, well laid-back, well laid-in, fitting smoothly into body. **Legs**—Straight, well-boned, muscular, set well-apart and under chest, with elbows set close to body. **Pasterns**—Strong, perpendicular. **Dewclaws**—May be removed. **Feet**—Firm, well-padded, point straight ahead.

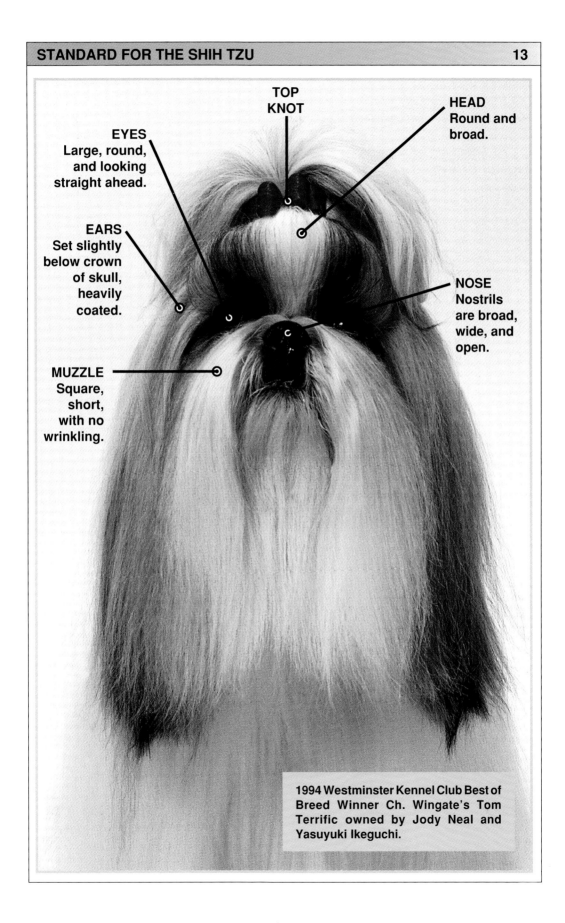

TOP KNOT

HEAD Round and broad.

EYES Large, round, and looking straight ahead.

EARS Set slightly below crown of skull, heavily coated.

NOSE Nostrils are broad, wide, and open.

MUZZLE Square, short, with no wrinkling.

1994 Westminster Kennel Club Best of Breed Winner Ch. Wingate's Tom Terrific owned by Jody Neal and Yasuyuki Ikeguchi.

Hindquarters—*Angulation of hindquarters should be in balance with forequarters.* **Legs**—Well-boned, muscular, and straight when viewed from rear with well-bent stifles, not close set but in line with forequarters. **Hocks**—Well let-down, perpendicular. **Fault:** Hyperextension of hocks. **Dewclaws**—May be removed. **Feet**—Firm, well-padded, point straight ahead.

　　Coat—**Coat**—Luxurious, double-coated, dense, long, and flowing. Slight wave permissible. Hair on top of head is tied up. **Fault:** Sparse coat, single coat,

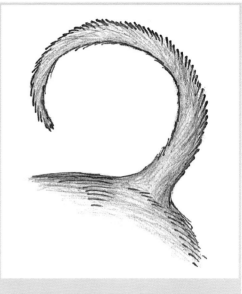

The tail carriage of the Shih Tzu is what is known as a pot-hook tail, where the tail is carried up and over the back. This is what it looks like underneath all the plumage. Drawing by John Quinn.

The great variation in color and markings makes each Shih Tzu a unique dog. A Shih Tzu with a considerable amount of white in his coat is considered flashy in the show ring.

curly coat. **Trimming**—Feet, bottom of coat, and anus may be done for neatness and to facilitate movement. **Fault:** Excessive trimming.

　　Color and Markings—All are permissible and to be considered equally.

　　Gait—The Shih Tzu moves straight and must be shown at its own natural speed, *neither raced nor strung-up,* to evaluate its smooth, flowing, effortless movement with good front reach and equally strong rear drive, level topline, naturally high head carriage, and tail carried in gentle curve over back.

　　Temperament—As the sole purpose of the Shih Tzu is that of a companion and house pet, it is essential that its temperament be outgoing, happy, affectionate, friendly and trusting towards all.

Shih Tzu come in a variety of colors, including solid black, all of which are equally acceptable in the show ring.

SHIH TZU AS A BREED

The Shih Tzu has a great many virtues which cannot fail to make it the small dog of the future. It is not a breed that can live alone in kennels, but one that delights in the company of human beings. Apart from its compact size, hardiness, soundness, and general good out that actual brain weight can be misleading as an index of intelligence; intelligence depends not so much upon quantity as upon quality, and this is dependent upon the structure and complexity of the brain. Nevertheless, it is an established fact that the Shih Tzu, in

Shih Tzu have a great many virtues that cannot fail to make them among the most popular of toy dogs.

temper, the Shih Tzu is remarkably intelligent. In common with the majority of the short-faced breeds, the brain size is relatively two-and-a-half times that possessed by any of the larger breeds, such as the German Shepherd or the Labrador Retriever. To be perfectly honest, one must point company with the Pekingese, the Pug, the Griffon, and other short-faced breeds, does possess a remarkable degree of intelligence. The Shih Tzu does not demonstrate its high intelligence in obedience trials, however, for these tests are, unfortunately, so designed that they inadvertently handicap the

This lovely portrait by Jeffrey Dali (nephew of Salvator Dali) is of Chumlari Trari. The artist has beautifully translated the charm of the Shih Tzu on canvas.

The bark of the Shih Tzu is not noisy yapping but rather a short, sharp bark that dwindles away into a series of throaty gurgles.

a hardy, sturdy little dog, slow to wear out, and able to carry on for many years without exhibiting signs of age.

It should always be remembered that the Shih Tzu is classed by the Kennel Club as a "Utility" dog and *not* a toy dog, whereas in the United States the breed is exhibited in the Toy Group.

A Shih Tzu will delight in a country walk. He is a hardy, sturdy little dog, slow to wear out.

Shih Tzu because of its small size, its inability to discriminate between closely allied odors, and the vision-obstructing hair that falls over its eyes.

The bark of the breed is also characteristic. There is no noisy yapping, but on special occasions one short, sharp bark that dwindles away into a series of throaty gurgles. It is given to neither expressing nor enjoying noisy outbursts of demonstrative affection, either from its owner or from admiring friends. But it will delight in a country walk and is

Apart from its compact size, soundness, and general good temperament, the Shih Tzu is remarkably intelligent.

YOUR NEW SHIH TZU PUPPY

SELECTION

When you do pick out a Shih Tzu puppy as a pet, don't be hasty; the longer you study puppies, the better you will understand them. Make it your transcendent concern to select only one that radiates good health and spirit and is lively on instinct. *Pick the Shih Tzu puppy who forthrightly picks you! The feeling of attraction should be mutual!*

DOCUMENTS

Now, a little paper work is in order. When you purchase a

A newborn litter of Shih Tzu pups. Young puppies sleep most of the time and usually are not available to see until a few weeks of age.

his feet, whose eyes are bright, whose coat shines, and who comes forward eagerly to make and to cultivate your acquaintance. Don't fall for any shy little darling that wants to retreat to his bed or his box, or plays coy behind other puppies or people, or hides his head under your arm or jacket appealing to your protective purebred Shih Tzu puppy, you should receive a transfer of ownership, registration material, and other "papers" (a list of the immunization shots, if any, the puppy may have been given; a note on whether or not the puppy has been wormed; a diet and feeding schedule to which the puppy is accustomed) and you are welcomed as a fellow owner to a long, pleasant association with a most lovable pet, and more (news)paper work.

GENERAL PREPARATION

You have chosen to own a particular Shih Tzu puppy. You have chosen it very carefully over all other breeds and all other puppies. So before you ever get that Shih Tzu puppy home, you will have prepared for its arrival by reading everything you can get your hands on having to do with the management of Shih Tzu and puppies. True, you will run into many conflicting opinions, but at least you will not be starting "blind." Read, study, digest. Talk over your plans with your veterinarian, other "Shih Tzu people," and the seller of your Shih Tzu puppy.

When you get your Shih Tzu puppy, you will find that your reading and study are far from finished. You've just scratched the surface in your plan to provide the greatest possible comfort and health for your Shih

The Shih Tzu puppy you pick should appear healthy, with bright eyes and a shiny coat.

Tzu; and, by the same token, you do want to assure yourself of the greatest possible enjoyment of this wonderful creature. You must be ready for this puppy mentally as well as in the physical requirements.

TRANSPORTATION

If you take the puppy home by car, protect him from drafts, particularly in cold weather. Wrapped in a towel and carried in the arms or lap of a passenger, the Shih Tzu puppy will usually make the trip without mishap. If the pup starts to drool and to squirm, stop the car for a few minutes. Have newspapers handy in case of car-sickness. A covered carton lined with newspapers provides protection for puppy and car, if you are driving alone. Avoid excitement and unnecessary handling of the puppy on arrival. A Shih Tzu puppy is a very small "package" to be making a complete change of surroundings and company, and he needs frequent rest and refreshment to renew his vitality.

THE FIRST DAY AND NIGHT

When your Shih Tzu puppy arrives in your home, put him down on the floor and don't pick him up again, except when it is absolutely necessary. He is a dog, a real dog, and must not be lugged around like a rag doll. Handle him as little as possible, and permit no one to pick him up and baby him. To repeat, *put your Shih Tzu puppy on the floor or the ground and let him stay there except when it may be necessary to do otherwise.*

Quite possibly your Shih Tzu puppy will be afraid for a while in his new surroundings, without his mother and littermates. Comfort him and reassure him, but don't console him. Don't give him the "oh-you-poor-itsy-bitsy-puppy" treatment. Be calm, friendly, and reassuring. Encourage him to walk around and sniff over his new home. If it's dark, put on the lights. Let him roam for a few minutes while you and everyone else concerned sit quietly or go about your routine business. Let the puppy come back to you.

Playmates may cause an immediate problem if the new Shih Tzu puppy is to be greeted by children or other pets. If not, you can skip this subject. The natural affinity between puppies and children calls for some supervision until a live-and-let-live relationship is established.

This applies particularly to a Christmas puppy, when there is more excitement than usual and more chance for a puppy to swallow something upsetting. It is a better plan to welcome the puppy several days before or after the holiday week. Like a baby, your Shih Tzu puppy needs much rest and should not be over-handled. Once a child realizes that a puppy has "feelings" similar to his own, and can readily be hurt or injured, the opportunities for play and responsibilities provide exercise and training for both.

For his first night with you, he should be put where he is to sleep every night—say in the kitchen, since its floor can usually be easily cleaned. Let him explore the kitchen to his heart's content; close doors to confine him there. Prepare his food and feed him lightly the first night. Give him a pan with some water in it—not a lot, since most puppies will try to drink the whole pan dry. Give him an old coat or shirt to lie on. Since a coat or shirt will be strong in human scent, he will pick it out to lie on, thus furthering his feeling of security in the room where he has just been fed.

HOUSEBREAKING HELPS

Now, sooner or later—mostly sooner—your new Shih Tzu puppy is going to "puddle" on the floor. First take a newspaper and lay it on the puddle until the urine is soaked up onto the paper. *Save this paper.* Now take a cloth with soap and water,

As Shih Tzu puppies grow, their fluffy puppy coat begins to develop into the luxurious, long, dense coat that is characteristic of the breed.

wipe up the floor and dry it well. Then take the wet paper and place it on a fairly large square of newspapers in a convenient corner. When cleaning up, always keep a piece of wet paper on top of the others. Every time he wants to "squat," he will seek out this spot and use the papers. (This routine is rarely necessary for more than three days.) Now leave your Shih Tzu puppy for the night. Quite probably he will cry and howl a bit; some are more stubborn than others on this matter. But let him stay alone for the night. This may seem harsh treatment, but it is the best procedure in the long run. Just let him cry; he will weary of it sooner or later.

Shih Tzu puppies are cute and irresistible! Choosing just one is always a difficult thing to do.

GROOMING THE SHIH TZU

It seems rather pointless to pay a lot of money for a purebred Shih Tzu and then neglect its grooming. Ten minutes a day is about all the grooming time your Shih Tzu will need. If it is done regularly, your pet can always be well-kempt, odor free and, at all times, looking his best. He will

The coat of the Shih Tzu carries a woolly undercoat, which appears more dense in the black and white than in the pure golden specimens. The coat should not be allowed to mat and if matting occurs try to separate it with the fingers.

The hair on the face and beard grows long. This is what makes its

The hair on the face and beard of the Shih Tzu grows long and hangs down on either side of the muzzle. This hair should be kept clean and be combed through regularly.

enjoy the feeling. Brushing will give him a pleasant tingling sensation and stimulate the flow of oil in his skin. He will appreciate being free of burrs and mats, and you will enjoy seeing the lustrous sheen that brushing promotes.

appearance so different from the Pekingese. At about ten weeks, hair starts to sprout outward on each side of the nose, giving a chrysanthemum-like effect—an unmistakable sign of the purebred Shih Tzu. When this hair grows longer, it should hang down on each side of the muzzle and should never be cut. The hair, which grows to considerable length, on the top of the head is brushed up and tied with a rubber band to form the typical topknot.

Some people prefer to let the hair hang down over the face, but there is a general belief that the eyes stay in better condition if exposed to light and air. So much hair generates heat and if it touches the eyes, ulcers may form. Eyes should be checked every day.

There is a dense "shank" of hair around the shoulders and patted down the back. The body coat often reaches the ground. The tail is carried gaily over the back to

The long hair on top of the head is brushed up and held together with a rubberband. If hair is left hanging down over the face touching the eyes, there is a greater potential for ulcers to form.

The Shih Tzu's coat should be parted down the middle of the back and brushed to hang evenly on both sides.

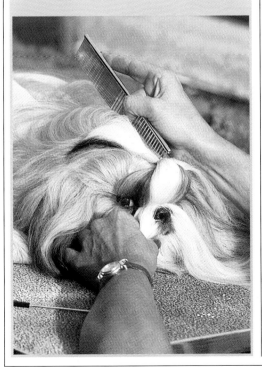

one side or the other. It should be plumed, not too tightly curled and, when brushed out, allowed to hang to one side or the other—not divided to hang equally on both sides.

The legs are strongly boned and heavily furred so that the legs are seen but not the feet. In China the dewclaws are left on as there is a saying that four dewclaws are lucky. These should be carefully trimmed, so as not to curl around in a circle and enter the flesh.

The gait of the Shih Tzu is free and flowing, with the hind feet thrown backward in movement,

When giving your Shih Tzu a bath, make sure to protect his eyes and ears from soap by applying mineral oil in the eyes and cotton in the ears.

Try to avoid giving a puppy a bath before it is six months old. You can, if the need arises, use one of the commercially prepared aerosol foam baths to give him a dry cleaning. With these, the foam is simply sprayed on, rubbed in and wiped off. Dry baths are also useful for grown dogs in damp or cold weather, or at times when a tub bath is impractical.

Choose a warm spot. The water temperature should be roughly the same as the dog's, which is about 101°F. A rubber hose shower spray (or a sprinkling can) will come in handy for wetting him down and rinsing him. Use a medicated

For quick trims, cordless grooming devices are available at your local pet shop. Photo courtesy of Wahl Clipper.

sometimes showing the pads of the feet. These pads must be watched as hair sometimes mats between the paws, and grit or small stones may get lodged between them and cause distress.

THE BATH

While dog experts argue about whether dogs should be bathed regularly or not, the fact remains that there are going to be times for hygienic reasons, if not for aesthetic ones, that your Shih Tzu will need a bath. Make it no more than once a month unless there's an emergency. Too frequent bathing removes beneficial oils.

To dry your Shih Tzu after a bath use an old bath or beach towel and rub him vigorously to stimulate the circulation.

Then wrap him in an old beach towel and rub him vigorously to stimulate the circulation. Particular care should be taken to dry the ears and feet, especially between the toes. A portable hair dryer can be used for the finishing touches, or, if one is not available, the dog could be vigorously exercised, indoors if it's cold out, outdoors if the weather is warm—but keep him on leash. Newly bathed dogs love to roll on the ground.

All the time you are bathing him make it a point to talk to him soothingly. If you make the first bath a game, you will have a lot less trouble with the later ones.

A hair dryer should be used to dry your Shih Tzu thoroughly. A dryer like this one attached to a table is convenient so that you can have both hands free to work the coat. Make sure the heat is not too hot—lukewarm is best.

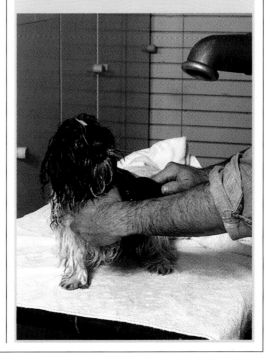

soap or shampoo formulated for dogs, working from the tail forward. Keep his head dry until the end of the bath because dogs usually don't shake until their heads are wet. Protect his eyes and ears from soap. Plug his ears with cotton and rub a little mineral oil or petroleum jelly around the eyelids.

Work the lather well down into the skin because that is where the real dirt is. Do not use soap on the head. Rinse lightly and then repeat the shampoo, as it is better to give two complete soapings, and if the dog is not then spanking clean, give a third.

Overdo the rinsing to make sure you get out every bit of soap.

FEEDING

Now let's talk about feeding your Shih Tzu, a subject so simple that it's amazing there is so much nonsense and misunderstanding about it. Is it expensive to feed a Shih Tzu? No, it is not! You can feed your Shih Tzu economically and keep him in perfect shape the year round, or you can feed him expensively. He'll thrive either way, and let's see why this is true.

First of all, remember a Shih Tzu is a dog. Dogs do not have a high degree of selectivity in their food, and unless you spoil them with great variety (and possibly turn them into poor, "picky" eaters) they will eat almost anything that they become accustomed to. Many dogs flatly refuse to eat nice, fresh beef. They pick around it and eat everything else. But meat—bah! Why? They aren't accustomed to it! They'd eat rabbit fast enough, but they refuse beef because they aren't used to it.

VARIETY NOT NECESSARY

A good general rule of thumb is forget all human preferences and don't give a thought to variety. Choose the right diet for your Shih Tzu and feed it to him day after day, year after year, winter and summer. But what is the right diet?

Hundreds of thousands of dollars have been spent in canine nutrition research. The results are pretty conclusive, so you needn't go into a lot of experimenting with trials of this and that every other week. Research has proven just what your dog needs to eat and to keep healthy.

DOG FOOD

There are almost as many right diets as there are dog experts, but the basic diet most often recommended is one that consists of a dry food, either meal or kibble form. There are several of excellent quality, manufactured by reliable companies, research tested, and nationally advertised. They are inexpensive, highly satisfactory, and easily available in stores everywhere in containers of five to 50 pounds. Larger amounts cost less per pound, usually.

If you have a choice of brands, it is usually safer to choose the better known one; but even so, carefully read the analysis on the package. Do not choose any food in which the protein level is less than 25 percent, and be sure that this protein comes from both animal and vegetable sources. The good dog foods have meat meal, fish meal, liver, and such, plus protein from alfalfa and soy beans, as well as some dried-milk product. Note the vitamin content carefully. See that they are all there in good proportions; and be especially certain that the food contains properly high levels of vitamins A and D, two of the most perishable and important ones. Note the B-complex level, but don't worry about carbohydrate and mineral levels. These substances are plentiful and cheap and not likely to be lacking in a good brand.

The advice given for how to choose a dry food also applies to moist or canned types of dog foods, if you decide to feed one of these.

Having chosen a really good food, feed it to your Shih Tzu as the manufacturer directs. And once you've started, stick to it. Never change if you can possibly help it. A switch from one meal or kibble-type food can usually be made without too much upset; however, a change will almost invariably give you (and your Shih Tzu) some trouble.

minerals are naturally present in all the foods; and to ensure against any loss through processing, they are added in concentrated form to the dog food you use. Except on the advice of your veterinarian, added amounts of vitamins can prove harmful to your Shih Tzu! The same risk goes with minerals.

For no-mess feeding, a feeding tray is very practical. Feeding trays are available in different colors and styles at your local pet shop. Photo courtesy of Penn Plax.

WHEN SUPPLEMENTS ARE NEEDED

Now what about supplements of various kinds, mineral and vitamin, or the various oils? They are all okay to add to your Shih Tzu's food. However, if you are feeding your Shih Tzu a correct diet, and this is easy to do, no supplements are necessary unless your Shih Tzu has been improperly fed, has been sick, or is having puppies. Vitamins and

FEEDING SCHEDULE

When and how much food to give your Shih Tzu? As to when (except in the instance of puppies), suit yourself. You may feed two meals per day or the same amount in one single feeding, either morning or night. As to how to prepare the food and how much to give, it is generally best to follow the directions on the food package. Your own Shih Tzu may want a little more or a little less.

Fresh, cool water should always be available to your Shih Tzu. This is important to good health throughout his lifetime.

ALL SHIH TZU NEED TO CHEW

Puppies and young Shih Tzu need something with resistance to chew on while their teeth and

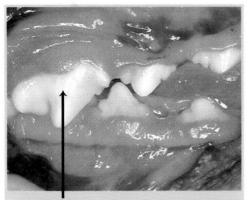

A scientific study shows a dog's tooth (arrow) while being maintained by Gumabone® chewing.

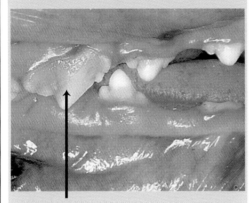

The Gumabone® was taken away and in 30 days the tooth (arrow) was almost completely covered with plaque and tartar.

jaws are developing—for cutting the puppy teeth, to induce growth of the permanent teeth under the puppy teeth, to assist in getting rid of the puppy teeth at the proper time, to help the permanent teeth through the gums, to ensure normal jaw development, and to settle the permanent teeth solidly in the jaws.

The adult Shih Tzu's desire to chew stems from the instinct for tooth cleaning, gum massage, and jaw exercise—plus the need

for an outlet for periodic doggie tensions.

This is why dogs, especially puppies and young dogs, will often destroy property worth hundreds of dollars when their chewing instinct is not diverted from their owner's possessions. And this is why you should provide your Shih Tzu with something to chew—something that has the necessary functional qualities, is desirable from the Shih Tzu's viewpoint, and is safe for him.

It is very important that your Shih Tzu not be permitted to chew on anything he can break or on any indigestible thing from which he can bite sizable chunks. Sharp pieces, such as from a bone which can be broken by a dog, may pierce the intestinal wall and kill. Indigestible things that can be bitten off in chunks, such as from shoes or rubber or plastic toys, may cause an intestinal stoppage (if not regurgitated) and bring painful death, unless surgery is promptly performed.

Strong natural bones, such as 4- to 8-inch lengths of round

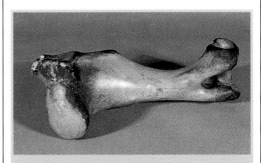

Pet shops sell real bones that have been colored, cooked, dyed or served natural. These are less safe than nylon bones.

shin bone from mature beef—either the kind you can get from a butcher or one of the variety available commercially in pet stores—may serve your Shih Tzu's teething needs if his mouth is large enough to handle them effectively. You may be tempted to give your Shih Tzu puppy a smaller bone and he may not be able to break it when you do, but puppies grow rapidly and the power of their jaws constantly

away from your dog when the teething purposes have been served. The badly worn, and usually painful, teeth of many mature dogs can be traced to excessive chewing on natural bones.

Contrary to popular belief, knuckle bones that can be chewed up and swallowed by your Shih Tzu provide little, if any, usable calcium or other nutriment. They do, however,

Gumabones® are probably best for your Shih Tzu puppy to chew on due to their softer composition.

increases until maturity. This means that a growing Shih Tzu may break one of the smaller bones at any time, swallow the pieces, and die painfully before you realize what is wrong.

All hard natural bones are very abrasive. If your Shih Tzu is an avid chewer, natural bones may wear away his teeth prematurely; hence, they then should be taken

disturb the digestion of most dogs and cause them to vomit the nourishing food they need.

Dried rawhide products of various types, shapes, sizes, and prices are available on the market and have become quite popular. However, they don't serve the primary chewing functions very well; they are a bit messy when wet from mouthing,

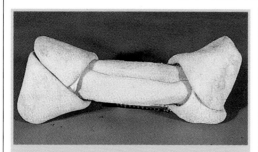

Rawhide is probably the best-selling dog chew. It can be dangerous and cause a dog to choke on it as it swells when wet.

and most Shih Tzu chew them up rather rapidly—but they have been considered safe for dogs until recently. Now, more and more incidents of death, and near death, by strangulation have been reported to be the results of partially swallowed chunks of rawhide swelling in the throat. More recently, some veterinarians have been attributing cases of acute constipation to large pieces of incompletely digested rawhide in the intestine.

A new product, molded rawhide, is very safe. During the process, the rawhide is melted and then injection molded into the familiar dog shape. It is very hard and is eagerly accepted by Shih Tzu. The melting process also sterilizes the rawhide. Don't confuse this with pressed rawhide, which is nothing more than small strips of rawhide squeezed together.

The nylon bones, especially those with natural meat and bone fractions added, are probably the most complete, safe, and economical answer to the chewing need. Dogs cannot break them or bite off sizable chunks; hence, they are completely safe—and being longer lasting than other things offered for the purpose, they are economical.

Hard chewing raises little bristle-like projections on the surface of the nylon bones—to

Molded rawhide, called Roarhide® by Nylabone®, is very hard and safe for your dog. It is eagerly accepted by Shih Tzu.

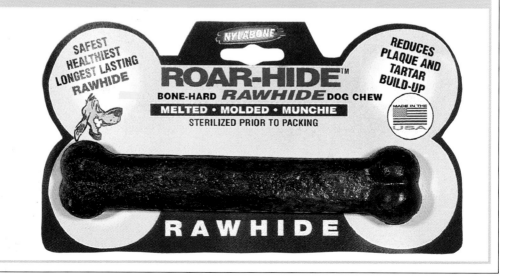

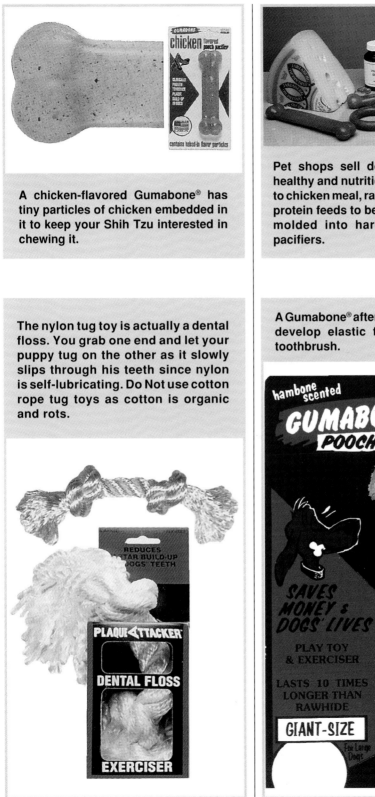

A chicken-flavored Gumabone® has tiny particles of chicken embedded in it to keep your Shih Tzu interested in chewing it.

Pet shops sell dog treats which are healthy and nutritious. Cheese is added to chicken meal, rawhide and other high-protein feeds to be melted together and molded into hard chew devices or pacifiers.

The nylon tug toy is actually a dental floss. You grab one end and let your puppy tug on the other as it slowly slips through his teeth since nylon is self-lubricating. Do Not use cotton rope tug toys as cotton is organic and rots.

A Gumabone® after chewing. The knobs develop elastic frays that act as a toothbrush.

provide effective interim tooth cleaning and vigorous gum massage, much in the same way your toothbrush does it for you. The little projections are raked off and swallowed in the form of thin shavings, but the chemistry of the nylon is such that they break down in the stomach fluids and pass through without effect.

The toughness of the nylon provides the strong chewing resistance needed for important jaw exercise and effectively aids teething functions, but there is no tooth wear because nylon is non-abrasive. Being inert, nylon does not support the growth of microorganisms; and it can be washed in soap and water or it can be sterilized by boiling or in an autoclave.

Nylabone® is highly recommended by veterinarians as a safe, healthy nylon bone that can't splinter or chip.

Nylabone® is frizzled by the dog's chewing action, creating a toothbrush-like surface that cleanses the teeth and massages the gums. Nylabone® pooch pacifiers, the only chew products made of flavor-impregnated solid nylon, are available in your local pet shop. Nylabone® is superior to the cheaper bones because it is made of virgin nylon, which is the strongest and longest-lasting type of nylon available. The cheaper bones are made from recycled or re-ground nylon scraps, and have a tendency to break apart and split easily.

Nothing, however, substitutes for periodic professional attention for your Shih Tzu's teeth and gums, not any more than your toothbrush can do that for you. Have your Shih Tzu's teeth cleaned at least once a year by your veterinarian (twice a year is better) and he will be happier, healthier, and far more pleasant to live with.

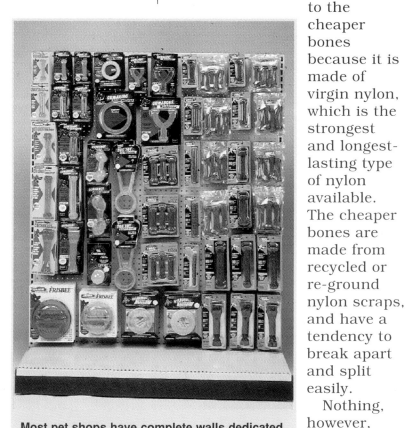

Most pet shops have complete walls dedicated to safe pacifiers.

The Gumabone® Frisbee®* has the advantage of a dog bone molded on top, making it easier for your Shih Tzu to pick up. *The trademark Frisbee is used under license from Mattel, Inc. California, U.S.A.

Nylabone® products come in many shapes and sizes, from bones to balls. The Nylaball® will be any Shih Tzu's favorite toy to chase.

An ideal snack for your Shih Tzu puppy is Chooz® by Nylabone®.This is a hard, molded bone of chicken and cheese. It exercises the dog's teeth, gums, and jaws while it also satisfies his appetite and need to chew.

TRAINING

You owe proper training to your Shih Tzu. The right and privilege of being trained is his birthright; and whether your Shih Tzu is going to be a handsome, well-mannered housedog and companion, a show dog, or whatever possible use he may be put to, the basic training is always the same—all must start with basic obedience, or what might be called "manner training."

Your Shih Tzu must come instantly when called and obey the "Sit" or "Down" command just as fast; he must walk quietly at "Heel," whether on or off lead. He must be mannerly and polite wherever he goes; he must be polite to strangers on the street and in stores. He must be mannerly in the presence of other dogs. He must not bark at children on roller skates, motorcycles, or other domestic animals. And he must be restrained from chasing cats. It is not a dog's inalienable right to chase cats, and he must be reprimanded for it.

Training should begin when your Shih Tzu puppy is still very young in order to ensure that you will have a well-mannered housedog and companion.

PROFESSIONAL TRAINING

How do you go about this training? Well, it's a very simple procedure, pretty well standardized by now. First, if you can afford the extra expense, you may send your Shih Tzu to a professional trainer, where in 30 to 60 days he will learn how to be a "good dog." If you enlist the services of a good professional trainer, follow his advice of when to come to see the dog. No, he won't forget you, but too-frequent visits at the wrong time may slow down his training progress. And using a "pro" trainer means that you will have to go for some training, too, after the trainer feels your Shih Tzu is ready to go home. You will have to learn how your Shih Tzu works, just what to expect of him and how to use what the dog has learned after he is home.

OBEDIENCE TRAINING CLASS

Another way to train your Shih Tzu (many experienced Shih Tzu people think this is the best) is to

Teaching your Shih Tzu to heel will make him much more amenable to walks. Heel means that your dog stays close to your left heel, not pulling to the left or right, running ahead, or lagging behind.

With patience and persistence, you can train your Shih Tzu to accomplish almost anything, such as competing in agility trials.

join an obedience training class right in your own community. There is such a group in nearly every community nowadays. Here you will be working with a group of people who are also just starting out. You will actually be training your own dog, since all work is done under the direction of a head trainer who will make suggestions to you and also tell you when and how to correct your Shih Tzu's errors. Then, too, working with such a group, your Shih Tzu will learn to get

Successful Dog Training is one of the better books by which you can train your Shih Tzu. The author, Michael Kamer, trains dogs for Hollywood stars and movies.

This Shih Tzu is learning the down/stay command in an obedience training class. Write to your national kennel club for details on training classes in your area.

along with other dogs. And, what is more important, he will learn to do exactly what he is told to do, no matter how much confusion there is around him or how great the temptation is to go his own way.

Write to your national kennel club for the location of a training club or class in your locality. Sign up. Go to it regularly—every session! Go early and leave late! Both you and your Shih Tzu will benefit tremendously.

TRAIN HIM BY THE BOOK

The third way of training your Shih Tzu is by the book. Yes, you can do it this way and do a good job of it too. But in using the book method, select a book, buy it, study it carefully; then study it some more, until the procedures are almost second nature to you. Then start your training. But stay with the book and its advice and exercises. Don't start in and then make up a few rules of your own. If you don't follow the book, you'll get into jams you can't get out of by must be your fault, since literally thousands of fine Shih Tzu have been trained by the book.

After your Shih Tzu is "letter perfect" under all conditions, then, if you wish, go on to advanced training and trick work.

Once your Shih Tzu has mastered basic obedience training, you may wish to go on to advanced work. This Shih Tzu is clearing the high jump in an obedience trial.

yourself. If after a few hours of short training sessions your Shih Tzu is still not working as he should, get back to the book for a study session, because it's your fault, not the dog's! The procedures of dog training have been so well systemized that it Your Shih Tzu will love his obedience training, and you'll burst with pride at the finished product! Your Shih Tzu will enjoy life even more, and you'll enjoy your Shih Tzu more. And remember—you *owe good training to your Shih Tzu.*

SHOWING YOUR SHIH TZU

A show Shih Tzu is a comparatively rare thing. He is one out of several litters of puppies. He happens to be born with a degree of physical perfection that closely approximates the standard by which the breed is judged in the show ring. Such a dog should, on maturity, be able to win or fun—yes, but it is a highly competitive sport. While all the experts were once beginners, the odds are against a novice. You will be showing against experienced handlers, often people who have devoted a lifetime to breeding, picking the right ones, and then showing those dogs through to their championships. Moreover,

Although showing your Shih Tzu is fun, it is a lot of work. You must learn how to show your dog to his best advantage.

approach his championship in good, fast company at the larger shows. Upon finishing his championship, he is apt to be as highly desirable as a breeding animal. As a proven stud, he will automatically command a high price for service.

Showing Shih Tzu is a lot of the most perfect Shih Tzu ever born has faults, and in your hands the faults will be far more evident than with the experienced handler who knows how to minimize his Shih Tzu's faults. These are but a few points on the sad side of the picture.

The experienced handler, as I

This proud Shih Tzu, surrounded by his trophies and ribbons, was in attendance at the World Dog Show in 1994 in Switzerland.

say, was not born knowing the ropes. He learned—*and so can you!* You can if you will put in the same time, study and keen observation that he did. But it will take time!

KEY TO SUCCESS

First, search for a truly fine show prospect. Take the puppy home, raise him by the book, and as carefully as you know how, give him every chance to mature into the Shih Tzu you hoped for. My advice is to keep your dog out of big shows, even Puppy Classes, until he is mature. Maturity in the male is roughly two years; with the female, 14 months or so. When your Shih Tzu is approaching maturity, start out at match

A wire crate such as this one comes in handy at dog shows for housing your Shih Tzu when he is not in the ring.

shows, and, with this experience for both of you, then go gunning for the big wins at the big shows.

Next step, read the standard by which the Shih Tzu is judged. Study it until you know it by heart. Having done this, and while your puppy is at home (where he should be) growing into a normal, healthy Shih Tzu, go to every dog show you can possibly reach. Sit at the ringside and watch Shih Tzu judging. Keep your ears and eyes open. Do your own judging, holding each of those dogs against the standard, which you now know by heart.

In your evaluations, don't start looking for faults. Look for the virtues—the best qualities. How does a given Shih Tzu shape up against the standard? Having looked for and noted the virtues, then note the faults and see what prevents a given Shih Tzu from standing correctly or moving well. Weigh these faults against the virtues, since, ideally, every feature of the dog should contribute to the harmonious whole dog.

"RINGSIDE JUDGING"

It's a good practice to make notes on each Shih Tzu, always holding the dog against the standard. In "ringside judging," forget your personal preference for this or that feature. What does the standard say about it? Watch carefully as the judge places the dogs in a given class. It is difficult from the ringside always to see why number one was placed over the second dog. Try to follow the judge's reasoning. Later try to talk with the judge after he is finished.

Ask him questions as to why he placed certain Shih Tzu and not others. Listen while the judge explains his placings, and, I'll say right here, any judge worthy of his license should be able to give reasons.

When you're not at the ringside, talk with the fanciers and breeders who have Shih Tzu. Don't be afraid to ask opinions or say that you don't know. You have a lot of listening to do, and it will help you a great deal and speed up your personal progress if you are a good listener.

THE NATIONAL CLUB

You will find it worthwhile to join the national Shih Tzu club and to subscribe to its magazine. From the national club, you will learn the location of an approved regional club near you. Now, when your young Shih Tzu is eight to ten months old, find out the dates of match shows in your section of the country. These differ from regular shows only in that no championship points are given. These shows are especially designed to launch young dogs (and new handlers) on a show career.

Traveling to dog shows with your Shih Tzu allows time for bonding. It is important for you and your dog to experience things together.

ENTER MATCH SHOWS

With the ring deportment you have watched at big shows firmly in mind and practice, enter your Shih Tzu in as many match shows as you can. When in the ring, you have two jobs. One is to see to it that your Shih Tzu is always being seen to its best advantage. The other job is to keep your eye on the judge to see what he may want you to do next. Watch only the judge and your Shih Tzu. Be quick and be alert; do exactly as the judge directs. Don't speak to him except to answer his questions. If he does something you don't like, don't say so. And don't irritate the judge (and everybody else) by constantly talking and fussing with your dog.

In moving about the ring, remember to keep clear of dogs beside you or in front of you. It is my advice to you *not* to show your Shih Tzu in a regular point show until he is at least close to maturity and after both you and your dog have had time to perfect ring manners and poise in the match shows.

YOUR SHIH TZU'S HEALTH

We know our pets, their moods and habits, and therefore we can recognize when our Shih Tzu is experiencing an off-day. Signs of sickness can be very obvious or very subtle. As any mother can attest, diagnosing and treating an ailment require common sense, knowing when to seek home remedies and when to visit your doctor...or veterinarian, as the case may be.

Your veterinarian, we know, is your Shih Tzu's best friend, next to you. It will pay to be choosy about your veterinarian. Talk to dog-owning friends whom you respect. Visit more than one vet before you make a lifelong choice. Trust your instincts. Find a knowledgeable, compassionate vet who knows Shih Tzu and likes them.

Grooming for good health makes good sense. The Shih Tzu's eyes need careful attention as they are slightly protruding and therefore prone to scratches and lacerations. Eye lids and lashes may be slightly irregular, and Shih Tzu commonly suffer from tearing problems, whether excessively or insufficiently.

The Shih Tzu's coat is double and long in length. The long outercoat benefits from regular brushing to keep looking glossy and tangle-free. Brushing stimulates the natural oils in the coat and also removes dead haircoat. Shih Tzu shed seasonally, which means their undercoat (the soft downy white fur) is pushed out by the incoming new coat. Mats and tangles in the Shih Tzu's coat can become very problematic: if you cannot commit to brushing this dog *daily,* have the coat clipped down. (Not to mention, floor-length coats need to be tied up to avoid becoming damaged during play and exercise.)

ANAL SACS

Anal sacs, sometimes called anal glands, are located in the musculature of the anal ring, one on either side. Each empties into the rectum via a small duct. Occasionally their secretion becomes thickened and accumulates so you can readily feel these structures from the outside. If your Shih Tzu is scooting across the floor dragging his rear quarters, or licking his rear, his anal sacs may need to be expressed. Placing pressure in and up towards the anus, while holding the tail, is the general routine. Anal sac secretions are characteristically foul-smelling, and you could get squirted if not careful. Veterinarians can take care of this during regular visits and demonstrate the cleanest method.

MAJOR HEALTH ISSUES

Many Shih Tzu are predisposed to certain congenital and inherited abnormalities, such as renal cortical hypoplasia, the most serious of these conditions which affects the kidneys, as well as thyroid malfunction, umbilical hernias and von Willebrand's.

Good health includes good grooming. The Shih Tzu's long outer coat benefits from regular brushing, which stimulates the natural oils in the coat and also removes dead haircoat.

Slipped stifles are a fairly common problem in the breed and can be corrected by a veterinarian through a painless procedure.

Shih Tzu also suffer from cleft palates and harelips, which are common congenital abnormalities seen in puppies. Cheiloschisis (cleft lip and harelips) is possibly by incomplete fusion of the upper jaw, can be surgically corrected if they are small; lips are corrected very early on, while palates may be corrected at around three months. Breeders commonly euthanize any puppies with gross defects.

Another puppy defect that Shih Tzu breeders are on guard for are

It is important to maintain your Shih Tzu's health from puppyhood to adulthood.

linked to nutritional deficiencies in the dam, or stresses or drug/chemical exposure. Cleft palates (palatoschisis) are found primarily in newborns and are likely hereditary, though there is some evidence to link them to ingestion of toxic agents, the use of steroids, or a virus. These defects, which are characterized stenotic hares or pinched nostrils, which pose breathing difficulty in six to eight week old puppies.

Eyes in the Shih Tzu, as we know, require much consideration. The breed is prone to eye ulcers as well as cherry eye. Cherry eye (known by veterinarians as prolapsed gland of the nicitans) appears as a red mass at the base of the eye (where the gland is enlarged). Surgery to "tack the gland down" will give relief to the affected animal, although the condition can recur and the surgery will need to be repeated. Shih Tzu breeders prioritize screening for eye problems.

Shih Tzu is a healthy, long-lived companion animal. Proper care and education can only help owners promote the health and longevity of their dogs. Most breeders advise against feeding the Shih Tzu one large meal per day because of the dangers of bloat (gastric torsion), the twisting of the stomach causes

The facial hair of the Shih Tzu grows outward in many different directions, earning him the nickname, "the chrysanthemum-faced dog."

Hypothyroidism (malfunction of the thyroid gland) can be linked to many symptoms in Shih Tzu, such as obesity, lethargy, and reproductive disorders. Supplementation of the thyroid decreases problems, though such dogs should likely not be bred.

Despite this lengthy list of potential problems, a well-bred

gas to build up and the organ expands like a balloon. Avoiding strenuous exercise and large amounts of water can preclude the occurrence of bloat, as can feeding two smaller meals instead of one larger one. A good commercial dog food is recommended for the dog's balanced diet.

VACCINATIONS

For the continued health of your dog, owners must attend to vaccinations regularly. Your veterinarian can recommend a vaccination schedule appropriate for your dog, taking into consideration the factors of climate and geography. The basic vaccinations to protect your dog are: parvovirus, distemper, hepatitis, leptospirosis, adenovirus, parainfluenza, coronavirus, bordetella, tracheobronchitis (kennel cough), Lyme disease and rabies.

Parvovirus is a highly contagious, dog-specific disease, first recognized in 1978. Targeting the small intestine, parvo affects the stomach, and diarrhea and vomiting (with blood) are clinical signs. Although the dog can pass the infection to other dogs within three days of infection, the initial signs, which include lethargy and depression, don't display themselves until four to seven days. When affecting puppies under four weeks of age, the heart muscle is frequently attacked. When the heart is affected, the puppies exhibit difficulty in breathing and experience crying and foaming at the nose and mouth.

Distemper, related to human measles, is an airborne virus that spreads in the blood and ultimately in the nervous system and epithelial tissues. Young dogs or dogs with weak immune systems can develop encephalomyelitis (brain disease) from the distemper infection. Such dogs experience seizures, general weakness and rigidity, as well as "hardpad." Since distemper is largely incurable, prevention through vaccination is vitally important. Puppies should be vaccinated at six to eight weeks of age, with boosters at ten to 12 weeks. Older puppies (16 weeks and older) who are unvaccinated should receive no fewer than two vaccinations at three- to four-week intervals.

Hepatitis mainly affects the liver and is caused by canine adenovirus type I. Highly infectious, hepatitis often affects dogs nine to 12 months of age. Initially the virus localizes in the dog's tonsils and then disperses to the liver, kidney and eyes. Generally speaking the dog's immune system is capable of combating this virus. Canine infectious hepatitis affects dogs whose systems cannot fight off the adenovirus. Affected dogs have fever, abdominal pains, bruising on mucous membranes and gums, and experience coma and convulsions. Prevention of hepatitis exists only through vaccination at eight to ten weeks of age and then boosters three or four weeks later, then annually.

Leptospirosis is a bacterium-related disease, often spread by rodents. The organisms that spread leptospirosis enter through the mucous membranes and spread to the internal organs via the bloodstream. It can be passed through the dog's urine. Leptospirosis does not affect young dogs as consistently as the other viruses; it is reportedly regional in distribution and

The Shih Tzu's eyes need careful attention as they are slightly protruding and therefore prone to scratches and lacerations.

somewhat dependent on the immunostatus of the dog. Fever, inappetence, vomiting, dehydration, hemorrhage, kidney and eye disease can result in moderate cases.

Bordetella, called canine cough, causes a persistent hacking cough in dogs and is very contagious. Bordetella involves a virus and a bacteria: parainfluenza is the most common virus implicated; *Bordetella bronchiseptica*, the bacterium. Bronchitis and pneumonia result in less than 20 percent of the cases, and most dogs recover from the condition within a week to four weeks. Non-prescription medicines can help relieve the hacking cough, though nothing can cure the condition before it's run its course. Vaccination cannot guarantee protection from canine cough, but it does ward off the most common virus responsible for the condition.

Lyme disease (also called borreliosis), although known for decades, was only first diagnosed in dogs in 1984. Lyme disease can affect cats, cattle, and horses, but especially people. In the U.S., the disease is transmitted by two ticks carrying the *Borrelia burgdorferi* organism: the deer tick (*Ixodes scapularis*) and the western black-legged tick (*Ixodes pacificus*), the latter primarily affects reptiles. In Europe, *Ixodes ricinus* is responsible for spreading Lyme. The disease causes lameness, fever, joint swelling, inappetence, and lethargy. Removal of ticks from the dog's coat can help reduce the chances of Lyme, though not as much as avoiding heavily wooded areas where the dog is most likely to contract ticks. A vaccination is available, though it has not been proven to protect dogs from all strains of the organism that cause the disease.

A well-bred Shih Tzu is a healthy, long-lived companion animal.

Rabies is passed to dogs and people through wildlife: in North America, principally through the skunk, fox and raccoon; the bat is not the culprit it was once thought to be. Likewise, the common image of the rabid dog foaming at the mouth with every hair on end is unlikely the truest scenario. A rabid dog exhibits difficulty eating, salivates much and has spells of paralysis and awkwardness. Before a dog reaches this final state, it may experience anxiety, personality changes, irritability and more aggressiveness than is usual. Vaccinations are strongly

COPING WITH PARASITES

Parasites have clung to our pets for centuries. Despite our modern efforts, fleas still pester our pet's existence, and our own. All dogs itch, and fleas can make even the happiest dog a miserable, scabby mess. The loss of hair and habitual biting and chewing at themselves rank

Although the long coat of the Shih Tzu is luxurious, it is a lot of work. Mats and tangles in the coat can be very problematic: if you cannot commit to brushing your dog daily, you may want to consider clipping the coat down.

recommended as rabid dogs are too dangerous to manage and are commonly euthanized. Puppies are generally vaccinated at 12 weeks of age, and then annually. Although rabies is on the decline in the world community, tens of thousands of humans die each year from rabies-related incidents.

among the annoyances; the nuisances include the passing of tapeworms and the whole family's itching through the summer months. A full range of flea-control and elimination products are available at pet shops, and your veterinarian surely has recommendations. Sprays, powders, collars and dips fight fleas from the outside; drops and

Shih Tzu have a "lap dog" personality;
they are not high-strung nor demanding
of attention.

pills fight the good fight from inside. Discuss the possibilities with your vet. Not all products can be used in conjunction with one another, and some dogs may be more sensitive to certain applications than others. The dog's living quarters must be debugged as well as the dog itself. Heavy infestation may require multiple treatments.

As for internal parasites, worms are potentially dangerous for dogs and people. Roundworms, hookworms, whipworms, tapeworms, and heartworms comprise the blightsome party of troublemakers. Deworming puppies begins at around two to three weeks and continues until three months of age. Proper

Although toy dogs, Shih Tzu love to spend time outside. Plenty of fresh air and exercise will keep your Shih Tzu in good health.

Always check your dog for ticks carefully. Although fleas can be acquired almost anywhere, ticks are more likely to be picked up in heavily treed areas, pastures or other outside grounds (such as dog shows or obedience or field trials). Athletic, active, and hunting dogs are the most likely subjects, though any passing dog can be the host. Remember Lyme disease is passed by tick infestation.

hygienic care of the environment is also important to prevent contamination with roundworm and hookworm eggs. Heartworm preventatives are recommended by most veterinarians, although there are some drawbacks to the regular introduction of poisons into our dogs' systems. These daily or monthly preparations also help regulate most other worms as well. Discuss worming

After your Shih Tzu has been playing outdoors, you should thoroughly check his coat for fleas and other parasites.

procedures with your veterinarian.

Roundworms pose a great threat to dogs and people. They are found in the intestine of dogs, and can be passed to people through ingestion of feces-contaminated dirt. Roundworm infection can be prevented by not walking dogs in heavy-traffic people areas, by burning feces, and by curbing dogs in a responsible manner. (Of course, in most areas of the country, curbing dogs is the law.) Roundworms are typically passed from the bitch to the litter, and the bitch should be treated along with the puppies, even if she tested negative prior to whelping. Generally puppies are treated every two weeks until two months of age.

Hookworms, like roundworms, are also a danger to dogs and people. The hookworm parasite (known as *Ancylostoma caninum*) causes cutaneous larva migrans in people. The eggs of hookworms are passed in feces and become infective in shady, sandy areas.

The larvae penetrate the skin of the dog, and the dog subsequently becomes infected. When swallowed, these parasites affect the intestines, lungs, windpipe, and the whole digestive system. Infected dogs suffer from anemia and lose large amounts of blood in the places where the worms latch onto the dogs' intestines, etc.

Although infrequently passed to humans, whipworms are cited as one of the most common parasites in America. These elongated worms affect the intestines of the dog, where they latch on, and cause colic upset or diarrhea. Unless identified in stools passed, whipworms are difficult to diagnose. Adult worms can be eliminated more consistently than the larvae, since whipworms exhibit unusual life cycles. Proper hygienic care of outdoor grounds is critical to the avoidance of these harmful parasites.

Tapeworms are carried by fleas, and enter the dog when the dog swallows the flea. Humans

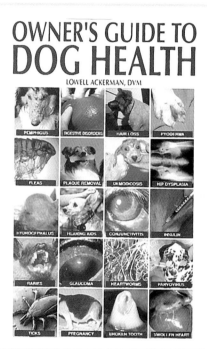

The undisputed champion of dog health books is Dr. Lowell Ackerman's encyclopedic work *Owner's Guide to DOG HEALTH*. It covers every subject that any dog owner might need. It actually is a complete veterinarian's handbook in simple, easy-to-understand language.

can acquire tapeworms in the same way, though we are less likely to swallow fleas than dogs are. Recent studies have shown that certain rodents and other wild animals have been infected with tapeworms, and dogs can be affected by catching and/or eating these other animals. Of course, outdoor hunting dogs and terriers are more likely to be infected in this way than are your typical house dog or non-motivated hound. Treatment for tapeworm has proven very effective, and infected dogs do not show great discomfort or symptoms. When people are infected, however, the liver can be seriously damaged. Proper cleanliness is the best bet against tapeworms.

Heartworm disease is transmitted by mosquitoes and badly affects the lungs, heart and blood vessels of dogs. The larvae of *Dirofilaria immitis* enters the dog's bloodstream when bitten by an infected mosquito. The larvae takes about six months to mature. Infected dogs suffer from weight loss, appetite loss, chronic coughing and general fatigue. Not all affected dogs show signs of illness right away, and carrier dogs may be affected for years before clinical signs appear. Treatment of heartworm disease has been effective but can be dangerous also. Prevention as always is the desirable alternative. Ivermectin is the active ingredient in most heartworm preventatives and has proven to be successful. Check with your veterinarian for the preparation best for your dog. Dogs generally begin taking the preventatives at eight months of age and continue to do so throughout the non-winter months.

Proper care and education can only help owners promote the health and longevity of their Shih Tzu.

SUGGESTED READING

OTHER SHIH TZU BOOKS

T.F.H. Publications, Inc., offers many quality books that all Shih Tzu fanciers can enjoy. *The Book of the Shih Tzu* (H-996) by Joan McDonald Brearly and Reverend D. Allan Easton contains important records and history of the breed from its early beginnings in the Orient up to its modern-day status all over the world. In this volume you will find a wealth of information essential to both the newcomer and the longtime fancier, plus hundreds of photographs presenting these enchanting "little lion dogs" in all their glory.

This Is The Shih Tzu (PS-661) also written by Joan McDonald Brearly and Reverend D. Allan Easton provides Shih Tzu owners with detailed and concise information from history to daily care and management of the breed. Beautifully illustrated with 170 photographs.

Both books will prove valuable additions to every Shih Tzu lover's library.

GENERAL DOG BOOKS

The following books are all published by T.F.H. Publications, Inc. and are recommended to you for additional information:

The Atlas of Dog Breeds of the World (H-1091) by Bonnie Wilcox, DVM, and Chris

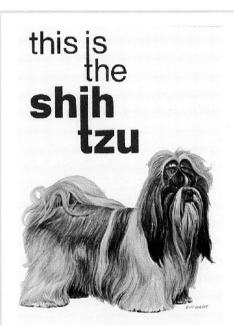

Reverend D. Allan Easton
Joan McDonald Brearley

Walkowicz traces the history and highlights the characteristics, appearance and function of every recognized dog breed in the world. 409 different breeds receive full-color treatment and individual study. Hundreds of breeds in addition to those recognized by the American Kennel Club and the Kennel Club of Great Britain are included—the dogs of the world complete! The ultimate reference work, comprehensive coverage, intelligent and delightful discussions. The perfect gift book.

Canine Lexicon by Andrew DePrisco and James Johnson, (TS-175) is an up-to-date encyclopedic dictionary for the dog person. It is the most complete single volume on the dog ever published covering

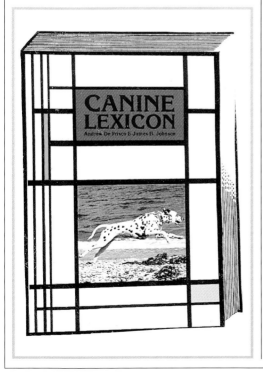

more breeds than any other book as well as other relevant topics, including health, showing, training, breeding, anatomy, veterinary terms, and much more. No dog book before has ever offered this many stunning color photographs of all breeds, dog sports, and topics (over 1300 in full color).

A very successful spin-off of the *Atlas* is *The Mini-Atlas of Dog Breeds* (H-1106), written by Andrew DePrisco and James B. Johnson. This compact but comprehensive book has been praised and recommended by most national dog publications for its utility and reader-friendliness. The true field guide for dog lovers.

Teaching the family dog has never been more fun and easy! *Just Say "Good Dog"* (TS-204) is a new approach in teaching dogs to be good family dogs and good house dogs. This most original manual to canine education by Linda Goodman, author and dog teacher, addresses all the basic commands and day-to-day problems as well as the considerations and responsibilities of dog ownership. Living with a dog should be a rewarding

experience, and this book will show you how. Delightful illustrations by AnnMarie Freda accompany the author's fun and anecdotal text to reinforce the importance of a positive approach to dog training. *"Just Say Good Dog"* is both very informative and authoritative, as the author, assisted by Marlene Trunnell, offers many years of experience and know-how.

Everybody Can Train Their Own Dog by Angela White (TW-113) is a fabulous reference guide for all dog owners. This well written, easy-to-understand book covers all training topics in alphabetical order for instant location. In addition to teaching, this book provides problem solving and problem prevention techniques that are fundamental to training. All teaching methods are based on motivation and kindness, which bring out the best of a dog's natural ability and instinct.

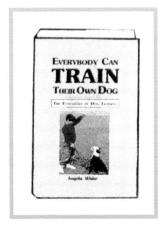